Kwanzaa

Seven Days of African-American Pride

Carol Gnojewski

Enslow Publishers, Inc.

40 Industrial Road	PO Box 38
Box 398	Aldershot
Berkeley Heights, NJ 07922	Hants GU12 6BP
USA	UK

http://www.enslow.com

Many thanks to Tasleem Qaasim and Yvonne Terrell-Powell
of Shoreline Community College for their inspiration and insight.

Library of Congress Cataloging-in-Publication Data

Gnojewski, Carol.
  Kwanzaa : seven days of African-American pride / Carol Gnojewski.
    p. cm. — (Finding out about holidays)
  Summary: Presents the history and meaning behind the observance of Kwanzaa.
  Includes bibliographical references and index.
  ISBN-10: 0-7660-2209-9
  1. Kwanzaa—Juvenile literature. [1. Kwanzaa. 2. Holidays.] I. Title. II. Series.
    GT4403.A2.G56 2003
    394.261—dc21

                                                        2003006849

  ISBN-13: 978-0-7660-2209-6

Printed in the United States of America

10 9 8 7 6 5 4 3 2

To Our Readers: We have done our best to make sure that all Internet addresses in this book were active and appropriate when we went to press. However, the author and publisher have no control over and assume no liability for the material available on those Internet sites or on other Web sites they may link to. Any comments or suggestions can be sent by e-mail to comments@enslow.com or to the address on the back cover.

Photo Credits: © 1999 Artville, LLC, p. 8; Bebito Matthews/Associated Press, pp. iii, 6, 38; © Corel Corporation, pp. 11, 14, 24, 29; Ariel Skelley/Corbis, pp. 4, 10; Associated Press, pp. 6, 32; Cheryl Wells, p. 42 (all); Clipart.com, pp. 5, 17 (all), 19; Damian Dovarganes/Associated Press, p. 9; Dave Scherbenco/Associated Press, pp. 12, 31; Ed Malitsky/Corbis, p. 7; Hemera Technologies, Inc., pp. ii, 13, 21 (all), 23 (all), 26 (all), 30, 34 (bottom two); James Leynse/Corbis, p. 25; Jim Cooper/Associated Press, p. 37; Karin Cooper/Associated Press, p. 35; Osamu Honda/Associated Press, p. 33; Photos.com, pp. 28, 34 (top); Susan Goldman/Associated Press, p. 36; The Star-Ledger, pp. i, 15, 16, 27, 39, 44, 45, 46, 47, 48; Tom Worner/Associated Press, p. 18; Warren Westura/The Star-Ledger, pp. 20, 43; William Perlman/The Star-Ledger, p. 22.

Cover Photo: The Star-Ledger (background); Karin Cooper/Associated Press (top inset); Photos.com (middle inset); © Corel Corporation (bottom inset).

CONTENTS

★

Kwanzaa lasts for seven days. It begins on December 26 and ends on January 1.

CHAPTER 1

Shared Harvest

At the end of the Western calendar year, there are many holidays. It is winter in the Northern Hemisphere. The days are very short and the nights are very long. In ancient times, people held winter festivals. Their festivals honored the New Year and the return of the sun.

At the close of the year in the United States, two big holidays follow one after the other. Christmas falls on December 25. New Year's Day is January 1. On these holidays, banks and businesses close. Mail is not delivered. Families gather to spend time with each other and to give each other gifts.

KWANZAA BENDERA

The black, red, and green bendera *(ban-DAY-rah) is the Kwanzaa flag. It is based on the flag created by Marcus Garvey, a black leader. The colors of the flag have a special meaning. Black stands for the people. Red stands for struggle. Green stands for future hopes. The flag is hung with the black stripe on top to show that people come first.*

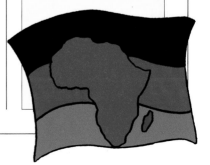

Dr. Maulana Karenga (right) continues to stay involved with African-American issues today.

Christmas is probably the biggest national and religious holiday. But for over 20 million people of African heritage, the day after Christmas is a source of joy and pride. Although it is not a federal holiday, December 26 marks the beginning of the festivities that last until the New Year. It is the start of a seven-day African-American harvest festival called Kwanzaa. During Kwanzaa, many African Americans practice the traditions of their ancestors far away in the Southern Hemisphere on the continent of Africa.

Like Christmas, Kwanzaa is a time of gathering and of giving gifts. But Kwanzaa does not take the place of Christmas. During Kwanzaa, African Americans celebrate all that they have in common with each other and with the people of Africa. Homes are decorated in bright African colors of black, red, and green. African clothing and hairstyles are worn. People greet each other in Swahili, a language spoken in most parts of Africa. *"Heri za Kwanzaa!* (HAY-ree sah KWAHN-sah)*"* they say. That means, Happy Kwanzaa!

During Kwanzaa, many restaurants and other public places are decorated in black, red, and green.

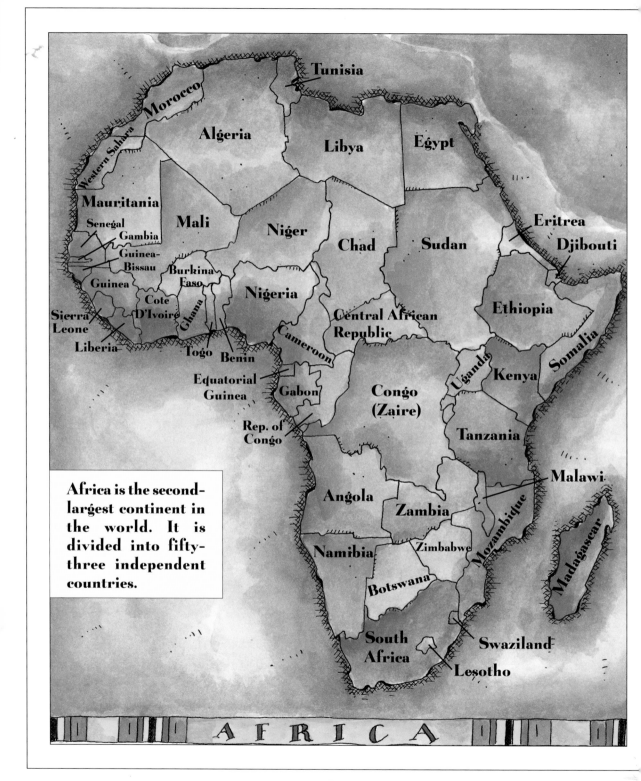

Morocco
Tunisia
Western Sahara
Algeria
Libya
Egypt
Mauritania
Mali
Niger
Chad
Sudan
Eritrea
Djibouti
Senegal
Gambia
Guinea-Bissau
Guinea
Burkina Faso
Nigeria
Central African Republic
Ethiopia
Sierra Leone
Cote D'Ivoire
Ghana
Somalia
Liberia
Togo
Benin
Cameroon
Uganda
Kenya
Equatorial Guinea
Gabon
Congo (Zaire)
Tanzania
Rep. of Congo
Malawi
Angola
Zambia
Mozambique
Madagascar
Namibia
Zimbabwe
Botswana
Swaziland
South Africa
Lesotho

Africa is the second-largest continent in the world. It is divided into fifty-three independent countries.

AFRICA

CHAPTER 2
A Brand-New Day

AFRICAN NAMES

★

Slaveholders often gave slaves new first or last names. One effect of this was a separation of the slaves from their own language and culture. In the 1960s, many black people did the opposite. They chose African names! This was a way of reclaiming their own language and culture. Dr. Karenga's birth name is Ron. His new first name, Maulana, is Swahili for "master teacher."

In Swahili, the word *kwanza* (KWAHN-sah) stands for "first." Kwanzaa is the first African-American holiday. An African-American teacher named Dr. Maulana Karenga created it. Although he borrowed many of his ideas from traditional African harvest festivals, the Kwanzaa holiday is very different. Dr. Karenga pieced together old and new rituals from Africa and the United States.

The Swahili phrase *matunda ya kwanza* (mah-TOON-dah yah-KWAHN-sah) means "first fruits." In Africa, first fruits refer to crops of food that are gathered or harvested at the end of the growing season. A "first fruits" harvest festival honors the land and all that grows each year. It brings people together to celebrate shared bonds of family and life. An example of a type of harvest festival is Thanksgiving. But Kwanzaa is about the gathering of people. African Americans come together to grow on the inside by learning, sharing, and remembering past achievements. Dr. Karenga and his friends held the first Kwanzaa celebration in 1966 in California.

Have you ever wanted to invent your own holiday? Take a moment to think about what that would be like. Planning a new holiday is a lot of work. Dr. Karenga had to answer

Kwanzaa is based on a traditional African harvest festival.

many tough questions. When would Kwanzaa be held? How many days would it last? Who would the holiday be for? How would people celebrate it? Dr. Karenga made these decisions and wrote them down carefully, so that others could follow his guidelines.

Holidays are repeated year after year. They should have lasting meaning. Do you think you could organize your beliefs to be at the center of a celebration?

Back in 1966, Dr. Maulana Karenga did. Dr. Karenga teaches African-American history at California State University in Long Beach, California. Creating Kwanzaa was his way of helping African Americans understand their

People of all generations celebrate Kwanzaa together.

rich history and culture. He wanted them to see their lives from an African point of view.

WHY DID DR. KARENGA CREATE KWANZAA?

It is important to those who celebrate Kwanzaa that others understand the culture and history of Africa and African Americans.

The United States is a democracy. In a democracy, everyone has a say in which laws get made, and the majority rules. When our country began, most voters were white men. Back then, most black people in America were slaves. Slaves had few rights.

But in the 1960s, many positive changes happened quickly in the black community. Because of the work of civil rights leaders, African Americans gained new freedoms, such as laws that protected their right to vote.

These leaders also taught African Americans how our country is run.

Black and white people now have equal rights, but some African Americans wanted an identity apart from white America. They wanted the power to make the laws for their own communities. Others wanted to form their own nation. But mostly, African Americans wanted to remember their history and respect their African roots. Dr. Karenga created Kwanzaa so that people would have a holiday that pays tribute to the African-American culture and identity.

Dr. Maulana Karenga

The landscape of Africa is very different from that of the United States. Much of Africa is made up of grassland like this, where giraffes, lions, zebras, and elephants live.

CHAPTER 3

Shared Beliefs

Dr. Karenga agreed that black people should take control of their lives and their communities. To build a stronger future, he knew that African Americans had to rethink who they were and what they wanted to be. Did they think of themselves as former slaves? Did they think of themselves as minority Americans? Did they think of themselves as a part of the African world?

In his own life, Dr. Karenga decided that "the first step forward is a step backward to Africa and African roots." He began to study African history. He traveled to many African countries

During Kwanzaa, gatherings may be held to teach others about the *Nguzo Saba*, or the seven principles.

and talked to people there. He learned how they lived and what was important in their lives. The wisdom he gathered became the *Nguzo Saba* (en-GOO-zoh SAH-bah).

The *Nguzo Saba* is a list of seven principles, or teachings, that African Americans celebrate during Kwanzaa. There are seven principles for the seven days of Kwanzaa:

 Day 1 *Umoja* (oo-MOH-jah): unity

 Day 2 *Kujichagulia* (koo-jee-CHA-goo-lee-ah): self-determination

 Day 3 *Ujima* (oo-JEE-mah): collective work and responsibility

 Day 4 *Ujamaa* (oo-JAH-mah): cooperative economics

 Day 5 *Nia* (NEE-ah): purpose

 Day 6 *Kuumba* (koo-OOM-bah): creativity

 Day 7 *Imani* (ee-MAH-nee): faith

Candles are an important part of the Kwanzaa celebration.

CHAPTER 4

The Kwanzaa Set

Planning for a holiday helps to set it apart from other days. It also puts everyone in a holiday mood. To prepare for Kwanzaa, families find a special place in their homes to display a set of seven Kwanzaa symbols. Some of these items will be used throughout Kwanzaa. Others serve as reminders of Africa. The seven Kwanzaa symbols are arranged in a certain way.

Would you like to make a Kwanzaa display? Here is what to do. First, find a mat. It can be a placemat, a tablecloth, or a piece of African cloth. Place your mat in the center of a table. The

KWANZAA SYMBOLS

The seven Kwanzaa symbols are:

mkeka (m-KAY-kah), or mat

mazao (mah-SAH-o), or fruits and vegetables

kikombe cha umoja (kee-KOM-bay cha oo-MO-jah), or unity cup

muhindi (moo-HEEN-dee), or corn

kinara (kee-NAH-rah), or candle holder

mishumaa saba (MEE-shoo-MAH-ah SAH-bah), or seven candles

zawadi (sah-WAH-dee), or gifts

mat will make a foundation. All the other symbols will rest on it.

Next, add some fruits and vegetables. Put them in a basket or a bowl. Or, set them directly on the mat. The fruits and vegetables are for the harvest. They also represent the rewards of work well done.

Many people make Kwanzaa displays during the holiday.

20

Corn is a separate Kwanzaa symbol. It is a grain that grows in South Africa. Each corn kernel is a seed that can be planted to grow more corn. To Africans, children are like seeds. They are the future. Collect an ear of corn for each child in your family. People who do not have children add an ear of corn to the display, too. In Africa, everyone in the community raises the children.

The unity cup is another Kwanzaa symbol. Family members drink together from this cup. This is done as an offering to the ancestors. Look for a special cup, such as one without handles. Many unity cups are made of wood or metals like silver or pewter.

Make room for a candleholder called a *kinara*. Keep it in a spot away from the cornhusks and other items that burn. Your

During Kwanzaa, a unity cup is used for offerings to the ancestors.

candleholder should be made of wood and hold seven candles. You will need one black candle, three red candles, and three green candles. The black candle is placed in the center. It stands for Africans and African Americans. Put the red candles on the left. They stand for the struggles of daily living. The green candles go on the right. Their green color stands for future hopes. Red candles are lit before green ones. This is to show that hard work and struggle lead to a better future.

Zawadi are gifts. Family gifts are the final Kwanzaa symbol. They can be homemade. They can be useful, like books. People usually give gifts made in Africa or bought from a store owned by African Americans. Wrap them in bright African colors.

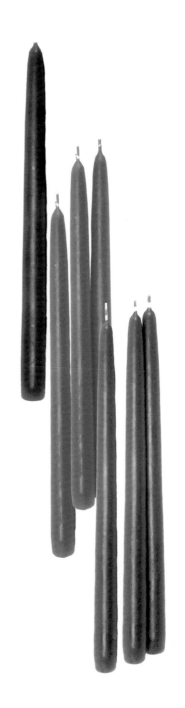

Hand-woven clothing is worn in Africa and also by many people in the United States.

CHAPTER 5
Celebrate Each Day

KENTE CLOTH

Kente (KEN-tay) is a type of cloth from the country of Ghana. It is made by sewing together long, brightly colored strips of hand-woven cotton. Shirts, pants, hats, dresses, and stoles made of kente are worn during Kwanzaa. The colors and designs woven into the cloth have special meanings.

December 26—Today is the first day of Kwanzaa. Light the black candle in the *kinara*.

"*Habari Gani* (Hah-BAH-ree GAH-nee)?" an adult will ask. "What's the news?" The response is "*Umoja*!" *Umoja* means unity.

Families, friends, and neighbors come together for *Umoja* night. In some communities, they meet at town centers, churches, or halls. Leaders and teachers make speeches. African drummers mark time on their drums. One of the leaders shouts "*Harambee* (hah-RAHM-bay)!" *Harambee* is a cheer. It is a call to pull together. Raise your right hand. Open your

fingers. Pull your hand down to your side and make a fist. Do this seven times. That is *harambee*. You are pulling together. Then, everyone lights a candle. They make a wish for the New Year.

December 27—Today is the second day of Kwanzaa. Light a black and a red candle in the *kinara*.

"*Habari Gani?*" The correct response is "*Kujichagulia!*" This means self-determination.

Everyone has his or her own way of doing things. Your attitudes and habits make up your lifestyle. The way you walk, talk, eat, and dress tells others who you are. Deciding what works best for you in your life is self-determination. Knowing what you like and dislike about your culture is also important.

During Kwanzaa, many people try out African clothing and hairstyles. What is African style? That depends. Africa is near the center of the earth. The sun's rays are hottest there all year round. In most parts of Africa, people wear dresses, T-shirts, and shorts just like we do in the summertime. But traditional clothing can be very different.

Ghana is a country in West Africa. On special days, men and women of Ghana drape woven cloth around themselves. Beads and other jewelry are worn on the body or braided into hair and clothes. Boys may wear *dashikis* (dah-SHEE-kees) or long, loose shirts. Flat, round hats called *kufis* (KOO-fees) may sit atop their heads. Some women wrap their heads

Many African Americans respect African culture by dressing in traditional clothes during Kwanzaa.

Tight rows of braids, like these, are known as cornrows.

with scarves. The wraps are called *geles* (GAY-lays). In Northern Africa, veils may be worn that cover the hair and face. Men there wear tight headpieces called turbans.

Braided hairstyles are common among black people worldwide. Tight rows of braids are called cornrows. False hair may be added to make the braids longer. Egyptian kings and queens wore wigs braided in long cornrows. Dreadlocks are another African hairstyle. They form when sections of hair are rolled up or left to tangle into stiff knots. The Jamaican singer Bob Marley made this hairdo popular.

December 28—Today is the third day of Kwanzaa. Light a black, red, and green candle in the *kinara*. "*Habari Gani*?" Today's response is "*Ujima*!" *Ujima* means collective work and responsibility.

For *Ujima*, families tackle household chores together, such as cleaning out a workroom or planning a spring garden. They may visit older relatives and help them clean or cook a meal. Some community centers offer classes for families. Health, safety, nutrition, and family games are topics that are taught.

Teenager Kenya Jordana James created *Blackgirl Magazine*. It is a good example of *Ujima*. Young black women all around the country read this magazine. They send in articles about themselves and the issues that are important in their lives. Similar online magazines and chat rooms allow children and teens to make friends and talk through problems.

December 29—Today is the fourth day of Kwanzaa. Light one black candle, two

Visiting older relatives during Kwanzaa is a good way to show you care.

red candles, and one green candle in the *kinara*. "*Habari Gani?*" Today, we respond, "*Ujamaa!*" *Ujamaa* means cooperative economics.

Money and wealth is a focus of this day. Families may save money all year to make a big purchase everyone will use, such as a couch, a TV, or a car. They shop at local stores where they know the owners. There are also *Ujamaa* Web sites on the Internet. They have links to businesses around the world that are owned by Africans and African Americans.

Camilla's Jam-N-Yams and Kelvis' Catering are two successful businesses owned by young black entrepreneurs. Jam-N-Yams is a pie company run by teenager Camilla White. She began her business when she was eight years old. Kelvis Patrick is a teenager who started a catering business. People hire him to make food for large parties and events. The BBQ and hot sauces he uses are his own special recipes.

Big cities like Chicago hold *Ujamaa* holiday markets. These are flea markets and arts and crafts fairs similar to the open-air markets found in African cities. African clothing, musical instruments, art, food, and handmade items are sold there. You will need to bargain to get the best price.

Sharing and being generous is another way to approach the day. Collecting food, clothing, and money for the poor is a rewarding *Ujamaa* activity. Some neighborhood groups try to think of ways to help out. They form carpools, babysitting clubs, and neighborhood watches. Others hold toy, book, tool, and jewelry swaps.

Forming food drives for needy people is one way of celebrating *Ujamaa*.

Dr. Martin Luther King, Jr., was one of the greatest American civil rights leaders. He showed people of all races how to live together in peace.

December 30—Today is the fifth day of Kwanzaa. Light one black candle, two red candles, and two green candles in the *kinara*. "*Habari Gani*?" People respond, "*Nia!*" *Nia* means purpose.

When do you feel most alive? What do you do that brings joy to others? These are questions family members ask each other on this day. All around us there are examples of people who make a difference in our lives. How do you show your thanks?

A roll call to the ancestors is a Kwanzaa ceremony that honors personal and historical heroes. An adult will begin by naming an important African or African American. It might be the name of a leader such as Sojourner Truth, Martin Luther King, Jr., or Kofi Annan. It may be the name of an artist such as Jacob Lawrence, or an inventor such as George Washington Carver.

Relatives who have passed away are also named. Anyone else who wants to may then name a hero and tell something about that person. How many famous African-American men and women can you name?

December 31—Today is the sixth day of Kwanzaa. Light one black candle, three red candles, and two green candles in the *kinara*. "*Habari Gani?*" Today, we say, "*Kuumba!*" *Kuumba* means creativity.

A *karuma* (kah-ROO-mah) is a harvest feast. Families try to be creative as they plan this big get-together. Most meals are potluck, which means each guest brings a dish. There are no set Kwanzaa menus, so families cook their own favorite recipes. Traditional

Kofi Annan is Secretary General of the United Nations.

Plantains are a kind of banana popular in African cooking. They may be served during Kwanzaa.

Potatoes and okra may also be found on the Kwanzaa table.

Southern foods, such as greens, sweet potatoes, and fried chicken are often served. Creole dishes, may be made such as a stew called jambalaya. African foods such as plantains, okra, and curried dishes may also be present. Hoppin' John, a Southern dish made with black-eyed peas, is said to bring luck in the New Year.

Before the meal, an elder will pour water from the unity cup into a bowl of lettuce or greens. The elder will spill the water four times, one for each of the four directions: north, south, east, and west. Then, he or she will make a toast to the ancestors and drink from the cup. The cup is passed around the table and everyone takes a drink. This ceremony is called *tambiko* (tahm-BEE-koh).

Although food is central to the *karuma*, it is

not the only party activity. There may be music and dancing. At the first Kwanzaa celebration, seven children performed a Kwanzaa skit. Families also exchange Kwanzaa gifts.

January 1—Today is the seventh day of Kwanzaa. Light all of the candles in the *kinara*. "*Habari Gani*?" The final response is "*Imani*!" *Imani* means faith.

The last day of Kwanzaa is a day of meditation. When you meditate, you are quiet and thoughtful. You think about your life and how you can improve it. Some families reflect upon the changes in their lives over the past year. There have been births, weddings, and funerals. People have moved away from or entered into the family. All these joyful and sad occasions are remembered.

Kwanzaa is a time for thinking and for remembering all the events that have occurred over the course of the year.

Traditional African songs and dances are popular during Kwanzaa.

CHAPTER 6

Come and Celebrate

RAP

Rap is a combination of music and poetry. It is one of many musical styles taken from Africa. Rap lyrics rhyme. They are spoken or chanted, not sung, to the beat. Creating a rap is a fun way to express joy and creativity during Kwanzaa.

Since 1966, Kwanzaa has grown from a small gathering of Dr. Karenga's friends and family in California to gatherings in many distant lands. From Africa to Canada, from Brazil to Barbados, people celebrate Kwanzaa.

In the United States, schools nationwide hold Kwanzaa programs. They include Kwanzaa among the winter holidays they teach each year. Public libraries have special programs for Kwanzaa. Storytellers tell African-American folktales, such as the Brer Rabbit stories. They also tell African folktales, such as those featuring Anansi the Spider.

Rapper LL Cool J

The Kwanzaa stamp, part of the Holiday Celebration stamp series, pays tribute to the African-American community.

Children's museums and zoos offer Kwanzaa activities and exhibits.

Kwanzaa has become more popular as years have passed. You can watch Kwanzaa movies and animated TV specials. You can buy Kwanzaa sets, cards, baskets, dolls, and even Kwanzaa candy bars. In 1997, the United States Postal Service issued a Kwanzaa postage stamp.

In the United States, anyone can invent a holiday. We are free to celebrate whatever we like. Cinco de Mayo, St. Patrick's Day, and Chinese New Year are other holidays that focus on just some of the many different cultures represented in our country. The First Amendment to the Constitution of the United

States guarantees the right of any group to gather peacefully for any reason.

Kwanzaa is a holiday created by and for African Americans. But it is also a holiday about family values. The teachings of Kwanzaa encourage respect for people of all colors. Dr. Karenga believes that the message of Kwanzaa is universal. "Any message that is good for a particular people," he says, "speaks not just to that people. It speaks to the world."

The message of Kwanzaa—respect for all people—lasts all year long.

Kwanzaa Project

★

Mancala Counting Game

Mancala is one of the oldest board games in the world. Most African tribes have their own special name for the game and their own ways of playing it. Today, *mancala* is popular all over the world. Like chess or checkers, it is a two-person game. You must think and plan ahead before you make a move. Play *mancala* with your family and friends during Kwanzaa!

You will need:

✔ **Empty egg carton**

✔ **2 plastic food containers**

✔ **48 small game pieces, such as beads, seeds, pebbles, or marbles**

1. Remove the lid of the egg carton. The bottom half of the carton is the game board. There should be twelve egg cups in all.

2. Place four game pieces in each egg cup. Game pieces can be any small items that fit inside the egg cups.

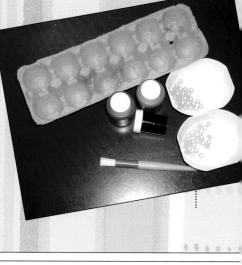

3. Set a clean, plastic food container on both ends of the egg carton. These are the *mancalas*, or game piece bowls.

4. Each player has one row of six egg cups. The *mancala*, or game bowl, to the right of each player is his or her game piece base.

To play:

1. The first player takes all the game pieces out of one of his or her six egg cups. He or she must then drop a game piece into the next cups to his or her right, following the board in a counter-clockwise direction. Drop just one game piece into each cup. The amount of game pieces you have in your hand tells you how many cups you will drop pieces into. For example, if there were four game pieces in the cup you chose, then you will place one game piece in each of four different cups on the board.

2. The *mancalas* also count as the cups you must drop the game pieces into. Game pieces can be placed into your own *mancala*. But do not drop your game pieces into your opponent's *mancala*.

3. The second player will then remove all the game pieces from one of his or her egg cups. He or she must also place one game piece in each cup on the game board in a counter-clockwise direction.

4. The game continues until one player's egg cups are empty. When this happens the other player removes all of the game pieces still in his or her egg cups and places them into his or her mancala.

5. Then both players count the number of game pieces in their *mancalas*. The player with the most game pieces wins the game.

Special Kwanzaa Rules: Any player who has seven game pieces in one of his or her egg cups may place all seven pieces in his or her *mancala*. Then he or she may take another turn.

Words to Know

★

achievement—Something that has been accomplished through hard work.

ancestor—Who a person is descended from.

community—People with common interests living together in a particular area or location or a group of people with common interests.

cooperative economics—Working together to build and maintain stores, shops, and businesses to profit as a community.

creativity—The ability to come up with or invent new things or ideas.

culture—The customs, beliefs, and ways of life of a group of people.

Words to Know

★

faith—For Kwanzaa, faith involves believing strongly in yourself, your abilities, and the community in which you live.

festival—A time of celebration.

group work and responsibility—To build and maintain a community together.

harvest—Gathering of crops.

hemisphere—Half of a sphere or globe. The equator divides planet Earth into its northern and southern hemispheres.

heritage—Traditions or property from earlier generations of ancestors.

identity—Who a person is.

principles—Values that guide people's actions.

Words to Know

★

purpose—Reason for doing something. The purpose during Kwanzaa is to make the community better.

self-determination—Making a decision to become who or what you want to be.

Swahili—An African language.

symbol—An object that represents or stands for an idea or thought.

tradition—The passing down of customs, stories, songs, or beliefs from one generation to the next.

unity—Being in agreement or harmony within a family, community, or nation.

Reading About

Brady, April A. *Kwanzaa Karamu: Cooking and Crafts for a Kwanzaa Feast.* Minneapolis, Minn.: Lerner Publishing Group, 1995.

Goss, Linda. *It's Kwanzaa Time!* New York: Penguin Putnam Books for Young Readers, 2002.

Murray, Julie. *Kwanzaa.* Edina, Minn.: ABDO and Daughters Publishing, 2003.

Internet Addresses

★

Everything About Kwanzaa
*Learn about the seven principles of Kwanzaa
and how the holiday began.*
<http://www.tike.com/celeb-kw.htm>

The Official Kwanzaa Web Site
*This informative Website features Kwanzaa facts,
decorations, gift ideas, and more.*
<http://www.officialkwanzaawebsite.org>

Index